HERE

ACKNOWLEDGEMENTS

This book would not have been written without the direct support of two remarkable people: Prof Alissa Trotz and Dr Anthony N Sabga, ORTT. Prof Trotz helped me more than she knows in in 2010, by securing for me the designation of Visiting Scholar to the University of Toronto. Dr Sabga was patron and benefactor in Trinidad, supporting in tangible and intangible ways, and placing a humbling confidence in me. I remain in their debt.

RAYMOND RAMCHARITAR

HERE

PEEPAL TREE

First published in Great Britain in 2013
Peepal Tree Press Ltd
17 King's Avenue
Leeds LS6 1QS
UK

ISBN 13: 9781845232122

Supported using public funding by
ARTS COUNCIL
ENGLAND

CONTENTS

For my mother, Dana
and
My daughter, Aurora

Death to the avant garde!
    — Derek Walcott

Life achingly said, *Do* something!
I didn't dare.
    — Frederick Seidel

HERE

Brahma sat on a lotus throne of sandalwood in a room at the end of a long hall and through a doorway set three steps beyond the end of the universe.

Indra entered. "You are to blame. It's your fault. All of it."

"Alas," said Brahma. "It is my loss that I ever created any of you."

"Ravana, the ten-headed Raksha king has wantonly slain my people," said Indra. "And you arranged that no one in heaven can kill Ravana. You set him over us all. He asked and you granted. Why? Just tell me why you grant boons to demons?"

"Oh, Indra, it was just an elusive impulse."

Ramayana *of Valmiki*

I

The *mise en scène* is a pastoral; a plain
rolling slowly across an island's torso,
its river's curves corseted by spines of cane,
marshland cut into squares by crooked fosses,
and jagged fractals dissolving the grass skin,
sprouting factory smoke stacks, then cilia
of mud and asphalt, the fragile veins joining
the clutches of huts, the overseer's white villa
to glints of glass and nickel, and the sheen
of neon and streetlights. Above the throb
of machines, the factories' exhalations, float
the ragged wefts of Bhojpuri prayers, coated
with films of incense, and the occasional sob
of lust for the Bharat of the Bollywood dream.

*

It is a kohl-ringed love, the golden eyes
set in almond orbits, cut with a primal
symmetry males are born to recognize –
eyes that could hold history, and apes, in thrall
standing at the factory gate on the fortnights
when labourers were paid. He took her home
to lamp-lit rooms and pall-draped mirrors. The lights
in her eyes brightened him more than the warm rum –
the peasant's cure for the blotted-out starlit wife,
the wound of a young son, and a wordless pain
he fingered mutely, and which he showed to me –
with fluorescent dreams of an electric life
flickering through the grief. Today, the skein
of dreams and the golden eyes still binds our three.

*

I cannot imagine my father a young man:
the one in pictures my daughter finds and points to
saying, "Daddy" – she cannot understand
how I was happier then, as she anoints
the sepia with a lavish little hand –
giggling at the grinning toff in pencil ties,
Sinatra's sharp-edged swagger, and eyes that spanned
the start of our forebears' deep-rooted enterprise
to its fruit he could only dream. But the snapshot
could not see the boy who had lost his mother,
who lived in the petticoats of remorseful aunts,
who wished, before he died, that he'd had a brother,
someone to trust, and protect him from the taunts
of golden eyes that ransomed love and comfort.

*

The Brahman girls of the '60s dressed like Jackie
Kennedy, and smiled like Norma-Jean;
the boys wore Brando and smiled matter-of-factly;
my mother said the clothes and smiles were a dream,
masks of the island Brahmans' Maya of Cabots
and Lodges; outside the illusion were morphine,
the nail-spiked clubs for labour unions, and garrotes
for heretics and dissenters from the divine,
who frothed at thought, like marriage, being controlled.
My father was not a Brahman, or Lodge, they said
when he came round, as Cary Grant with dreamy
eyes, but he was bright, and would get ahead.
She saw the dream, the desperate fleck of gold,
and understood, and the Cabot accepted the Sweeney.

II

A dream: a poem that sounds like a warning –
Seidel's "The Sickness", which ends on Eighty-Sixth
Street, near the Park, one ordinary morning:
an early soubrette, a fuming bus, a fixed

Routine. In this dream, there's nothing to do for hours
'til the Met opens – what draws me there is always
the same: the Egypt exhibit, the Sphinx that glowers
knowingly, Pharaoh, Anubis, the Hebrew slaves

Who etched the scallops in each gryphon's wing –
the spectacle of God's chosen people at slaughter –
courtesy Cecil B. DeMille, presenting
Charlton Heston in a skirt, while Pharaoh's daughter,

Anne Baxter, and her maids, fretted in Technicolor.
I begin there, in New York, or there, in Egypt.
Anywhere, you might say, but *here*, in duller
light, and an obscurer story, where the whip

Played the starring role, and often still does.
So I'd better get to it; there are still fields
that remember the mud between the forlorn toes
that threaded furrows, behind the iron wheels

Of oxcarts pregnant with cane-stalks, and whispered
Bhojpuri curses beneath acidic breath,
or love poems – whatever came through the blistered
betel-stained lips stank of violence, threat.

Then evenings, on dirt floors swept with palm fronds,
the oiled joints of tawny bodies squatting outside
the smoke-blackened tin-roofed barracks, murmuring songs,
low and primal, smooth rum, bhang, then the slide

13

From history into the samadhi state,
gazing at the saffron-faced horizon
where black-limbed havan smoke hung frozen, in wait
for the haughty Aryan gods to realize an

Offering had been made, then coaxing them
with tears and music, but they never came,
and the whispered strophes dissolved into pablum.
The blue-skinned gods were stunned by shame

That ten million fierce-moustached kshatriyas armed
with the Vedas, fed by the headwaters from Shiva's
topknot, could be effortlessly damned
by a hundred thousand chinless, blue-eyed reavers,

And they pretended not to see the havans
that flowered from the lonely Caroni Plains
in fragrant ghee, or hear the plaintive bhajans
that wavered like the flickers of wood-torch flames.

The slender, manicured nails slowly grazed
the indigo chins, as they lounged in Indra's demesne,
and wordlessly the mercuric eyes blazed
assent, like jewels in velvet: *sudras weren't men*.

And left them to diabetes, uxoricide,
and a thick-fingered crushing boredom, whose cure
was ganja, rum, the Manas, a child bride.
They took a century and a half to find the door

Out of those fields, and god knows how much more
to forget them.
                                    So much for history.
You could still see the cane fields from our
back porch as late as the 80s. By then the mystery

14

Of the rough-edged past had become a silky fetish,
and you saw the younger coolie doctors in koortahs
and heard the tinny music, and felt the rush
of memory incarnating Hema and Mumtaz

As Sita and Parvati, invoked and worshipped
every Wednesday in the Hylite drive-inn,
when they let coolies in by the carload, and slipped
them fliers for yagnas and satsanghs – the hives in

Which their droning could meet, mingle and multiply,
like the accordion folds that wheezed the mournful
melodies that softened the strophes from the dry
epics – as penance for the indulgence in scornful

Lowbrow peasant leelas, where Amitabh
and the crooning, fair-skinned Bollywood simulacra
were molecules, dancing to dissolve the drab
barrack compound, so coolies could remake a

A gold-leafed pastoral, with devas in brass,
and bestiaries of Aryan-animal hybrids.
The gods became works of art in the age of mass
reproduction – an orgy of eyes and limbs on all sides,

Oozing the pink-skinned beauty peasants crave;
the sapient sadhu became a hedonist
decked in organza and tulle, as he traced the grave
ash on each forehead, the sacred thread on each wrist;

And they brought the robed charlatans from Bharat
to babble the Sanskrit words, as they fed Agni
the ransom, and petition for a new concordat
for a New World. The gods considered the sagging

Clouds, heavy with gold bibelots the peasants
offered, like a low-born lover offers stars,
then laughed a little: the coolies were like infants.
Heaven had changed after an age of wars

And only fragments of their magic remained:
the prayers, offerings, and flags were mere ornaments
now. They'd grown bored, the epics had become mundane
and kingdoms of stone and magic dwindled like incense.

But the robed charlatans, the sacred thread
and the offerings to Agni, now properly proffered,
had to be honoured. They stirred, sighed and bled
their ichor into the ether, and prepared to suffer

A final, absurd round of incarnations
to walk the improbable spaces of crumbling Maya,
near her navel, in those far-flung stations
where their lost children sat, drunk and crying.

But in the profane cane fields, the peasant body
could not practice austerities, was too enmeshed
in the syrupy world; avatars became godly
satyrs whose immanence succumbed to flesh.

I remember Hanuman, the monkey god,
in the body of a red-eyed government clerk
who carried a flask in his back pocket. He would
caress the bottle's curves and complain about work,

His children, his wife, Ravana's ugly sister
as his breath roared, his furious heart heaved
with rage, then laughter, then tears, as he choked, then kissed
the bottle's neck, as he dreamed of how to deceive her

Into taking the children and leaving forever.
Giggling, splitting the human face apart
at moments, as the liquor burned to sever
the monkey's laughter from his stubborn heart.

Every day, I passed by Ram who beat
the gold-skinned Sita bloody, but she stayed,
and Lakshman who staggered down the main street
sometimes at night, singing, unafraid,

Of the marigold faces of trembling peasant girls
whose fathers, enflamed at night by spirituous fires,
consumed the innocence spun in the whorls
of petal-soft cheeks, and crushed them into Apsaras.

The older women understood the words
and shook their silver-streaked heads; some cried a little
and would never say why. These instants were the surds
etched on the veils of a karmic joke, the riddle

We lived in – a fragrant island of neon, afloat
on black water, a Republic of smoke
ruled by a white-masked god with a black-skin coat
where slant-rhymed heroic couplets deposed the sloka.

III

Vishnu thinned hair and lips to become a Samajist
and uncle. He drove me to school in his Hillman Minx,
unravelling the mysteries in every twist
of the road to Carli Bay, as the sea blinked

Through the gauzy tassels trailing the shafts
of the cane arrows erupting from springy leaf
calyxes, and I bounced on his horse-laughs
as he spoke fondly of Odysseus, the thief

Who relieved Polyphemus of his eye;
Arthur, who inveigled Excalibur from stone;
Apollo, whose Cadillac chariot blazed the sky;
and rose-lipped beauties biding in every crone.

In the village school where he was Raj and prelate,
the sunburnt vassals, with dim eyes and callused palms,
offered their clear-eyed children to a lighter fate
through the salvation of his sheltering arms.

I don't know if the children ever grew up,
or if around the innocent, adoring eyes
were lambskin masks that hid a cold, corrupt
desire that used the books, and prayers, to disguise

Its intent: to lacerate the smooth green
of the fields, to strangle the moody, insatiable sea
that haunted them and swallowed every dream
that lived in the word they traced in the sand: *free.*

Free from the tireless cartwheels of rebirth,
free from its red-ink laws and karmic bonds
the weary ships drew tighter around the girth
of the old world, and their quicksand desponds

Known in other worlds as *boredom.* The cure
was faith in a single death and final rebirth
whereupon the souls who'd been certified pure
would claw triumphantly out of the dirt.

It was enchanting: the thought of vast sound-stages
on the Caroni plains, the thousand-limbed
forests as extras, with Rakshas and white-haired sages
to tend the ancient spools that wound the film

Of life after life, and gods for every moment –
to spin those maelstrom lives to a single gyre
of one story, all the pain to a single lament,
was, for those crushed by the wheel of life, inspired.

"Don't believe the nonsense about prayer and fasting,"
he said, one day, in a moment of anger. "You know
in India, a brahman saw a beggar passing.
The man asked for food, but dharma did not allow.

The brahman saw the same man the following day,
dead, and thought, 'He is gone back to be reborn'.
But suddenly he realized, 'I say
what I've been taught. It is useless to mourn

The dead. They return to a station their
Karma dictates. But suppose there is no spirit?
What if all we can hope to achieve is living here?
What if the Law of Karma is Brahmanic shit?'"

He laughed as he said it, a little cruelly.
Early in his life, he'd shown promise
and was taken from it, away from the unruly
rage of bejewelled gods, and the razor-tongued bliss

Of rum gave way to the red-faced impatience
of Irish priests, whose prickly brogue knit fear
as they forced the coolies to their knees for stations
of the Cross, as prelude to the tortures of Shakespeare

And Homer. The grimness of the priests had gone
by like visions Christ contrived in the desert,
by the time he unravelled the *Odyssey* along
the Byzantine Carli Bay Road. I saw their worth

Only much later. He took an age to die,
holding on to life because he knew
the void awaited, his soul would not fly
to Samsara, but evaporate like the dew

On the stolid canes, and his children would amount
to nothing. Even his dreams could provide no harbour
as he watched them flower, then fade and fall into gaunt
middle age, and the lurid cult of Sai Baba.

I remember him since I, too, sidestepped the mud.
By then, pink priests had been replaced by dark
votaries in white habits, converts who would
console the new Republic, where the black clerk

Had straightened his back and become the Black Master
whose sins could only be heard by a Black Confessor.
The College of Our Lady of Disaster
was history's white-faced diamond, its impresa

On the fallow fields, set in dogmatic concrete.
The Virgin took the best of the peasants' litters
and infected them with the virus of conceit
to set them, like brown Adams, above the creatures

Of the field, who galumphed across the earth and made
its machines run, who spirited rum, and killed
their wives. We would be siddhis for which they prayed –
the crystals that had grown in the humid, stilled

Suspension of lonely plains, emptied of oxcarts
and the swish of cutlasses cleaving the spindly shanks
of cane, and of loose-limbed bodies that moved like larks
moved through love poems. In truth, we were blanks

In khaki trousers and white shirts, blinking
at the precision of the quadrangle, the strict
order of the lawns, and curious sprinkling
of boys in stark black skins, being slowly mixed

Into our flock by stony Shepherds whose virtue
was that they, too, had sat in the steel and ply
chairs, and watched old masters bring new
light to old mystery in the dark chalkboard eye

Whose retina etched it all: the Black Power
fists in the 70s, the black scuts in the shaved
heads, as the coolie renaissance began, and flowered.
The Shepherds and dark monks remained enslaved

By Our Lady of Inertia, by whose grace
Newtonian mechanics and the calculus
prevailed, and left the frozen marble face
unlined by time, like our prosaic prospectus –

The mantissa of Indenture – who could achieve
Nirvana as doctors, lawyers, scientists.
But when *our* time had come to be deceived
an era folded as our Holy Father Narcissus

Died. The physics changed with the atmosphere.
The Shepherds retreated into broken spines
of old texts, whose dogma withered in the new air;
their stories faltered, and Fordist assembly lines

Stuttered. Clermont, the giant whose biceps split
his sleeves, began to wear open-toed sandals
and mixed basic math with relativity;
he told us stories of youth, girls, and scandals

Always averted by leaden morals: *hold off, wait* –
the catechist's cure for our youth – *atrophy*.
And we saw the malaise in its advanced state
in Satra, the Jain who taught geography

And tried to sell us school supplies. "You know,"
said Singham, the science man, "you fellers are lucky
to be here." As obvious as gravity, as if no
more needed saying, no effort to unlock the

Theorems of Black Nationalism, or Boy George
dressing like a girl, or how Michael Jackson
conquered the moon, or the cowboy frenzy that surged
through the old empire, launching attacks on

The value of art. The college became the Church
of the Machine, and we its acolytes,
groomed to look down from glass windows, perched
atop new factories, manned by troglodytes,

Our brothers. Bureaucrats did not need the arts –
what use were the sly seraphs of literature
in factories to calibrate missile parts?
Softness was too much light for a creature

Bred for the earth's dark places. Orthodoxy,
decreed in the New CXC syllabus,
erased the traces of Wells, Orwell, Huxley
and replaced them with Montesinos and las Casas.

And thus released from the hair shirts of tradition
we careened into the waiting idle hands
of the world outside, the Creole conurbation
whose vice, and music, and laughter, were Caliban's —

The anti-hero, born in another epic
I would learn later: The father of the Other
race, who were not accounted for in the mystic
texts, and whom history, they said, had tried to smother

In the crib. We were taught his picaresque story —
one with no heroes, morals, or cities of gold
but catalogues of grief and former glory
he made, which were stolen by the world.

IV

The Creole genesis was the war of half-light
against dark: No caprice of red- and blue-skinned gods
spun lives out of orbits, no day and night
of death and rebirth, no endless circular quods

That spun into a never-ceasing wheel.
The plot was simple: the soul, lost in darkness;
one book, one creed, one Saviour would reveal
the eternal light, along a path marked with

The blood of a blond lamb, or curried scapegoat.
Their parables were sung in rhyming couplets —
the lyrics raucous, carnally wet and bloated,
descrying bodies and faces skimmed by droplets

Of sweat of the high brought low in the travails
common to all faiths, even the most sublime.
Its *primum mobile* was three caravels,
a shipwreck, a virgin beach, and a founding crime.

The master was a bearded, straight-nosed Titan,
who made the Creole Caliban in his image
seen in rippling water: odd-shaped, uncertain,
entranced by the sea, and veined with runnels of rage

And lust for alabaster Miranda, the blue-eyed
daughter, who watched her father's shadow-heir
hew wood and draw water for the drunken crew,
and later, in muggy, limp-leafed evenings, clear

The Titan's cloudy moods at being trapped
in the isle of noises, whose heart was a steel drum
that deadened cicadas' throbbing tongues and the lap
of prying white-tongued waves, and drowned the hum

Of the spirit, Ariel, his invisible servant,
who greedily dreamed of the end of his indenture
when, visible and immovably seated on the verdant
plain, he could stake his claim to the frontier —

Dreaming of gods and colours he would bring:
another music, another desideratum.
But in this story there is no Second Coming:
only the present: The Worldly Now is the Kingdom,

And every Creole a priest and prophet, an expert
in Apocrypha, their gospels thrilling and legion,
and elastic enough to sling the hesitant convert —
like the malleable Manas, stories changed with region

And audience and apostle. Mine was Jude
the Oblique, who attended the college chapel
with convert college boys. He laughed at our crude
hairstyles and bell-bottomed trousers, as we grappled

With the Creole creed, through Smokey Robinson,
and the sterile mystery of the Virgin Birth.
"I don't like college fellers," he said. "Not one
lick down a sweet salt-meat or play a shit-worth

Of football," – in between the monotonous chants
from the sweat-smoothed pages of the catechism.
We could accept the Body of Christ in our hands
or on the tongue. The ritual seemed gruesome –

To offer a man his tongue – and he pressed his lips
to a thick line and stretched his work-dark palms
upward, caressing the Host, and gently sipped
the wine. He settled, lupine amongst lambs

At Communion, and offered me the sign
of peace. He took my umber, flaccid hand
in his worldly grip, and said: "Your peace is mine,
and mine is yours." I was awed by the grandeur

Of the gesture, and said, without knowing why:
"You will always be my friend." They weren't
my words. In *The Wrath of Khan*, about to die,
Spock's final thought to Kirk, in the charged moment

Was: "I am, and shall always be, your friend."
A cartoon bubble from mouths of comic creations
of a distant mind, on the fringes, past the end
of history, the sublime imagination's

Outhouse – where men had gone, and returned with tales
of forests, bestiaries, and gold, but no people
in any sense of the word – just wild-eyed Ishmael's
and rapine Ravan's litters, dull and gullible.

He laughed at me; I aped him and learned laughter.
I followed him to Motown, and copied the chords
of the Creole tongue, its joyous lilt, its softer,
dreamy logic, and mimicking his goads

I learned to speak. He enjoyed my aping him –
the voice, the obscene Superfly swagger. "You learn
too fast, just now you go want to wear my skin."
His skin, and the vista inside, were all he owned.

He furnished it with a broad, star-littered sky,
a Palladian mansion, and pale-blue airy rooms
for a mother, brothers, sisters, an absent, sly
father he revered, who came and went with the moon's

Conscience: blooming for a time, like love,
but every day fading, falling, dying.
Outside the castle of his skin, he moved
on earth like the Angel of Gleeful Noise, flying

Lightly across the angry factories, or knocking
around the seamy standpipe duels and jokes:
She tell me how your mouth taste like my cock.
Then floating into razor-seamed soutane cloaks,

Mixing laughter and flour: "I like the shit
when people try to fuck with me," – the round
face, the brick-edged jaw, the perverse sunlit
smile, the hematite halo of Caliban's crown.

"The more they fuck with me, the better I get,
like Rocky and the Russian, I win in the end…"
He spoke like a Viking emptying a goblet,
like a fake eunuch strutting through a harem,

A deposed prince exiled on a food-stained
couch on Saturday mornings, watching videos,
while his mother, arraigning the house, rained
sunshine: "Yeah, train for the fight, I go feed your

Hungry arse. You could fight any Russian?
Try and make a few rounds with them schoolbook
nuh." Her voice, her treelike thighs, could crush an
idle thought like, somehow, avoiding the hook

Or crook that brought her children the good life.
She despaired for him: his unrequited thunder
outside of resonant valleys would find only strife
in the flat-featured plains, and it burned her

That his fury would never be harnessed, only feared
and grounded for life on a factory floor –
a leaden, windowless destiny, ensphered
in the orbit of old ideas, still enamoured

With dreams of shipwrecks, and creaking iron wheels
where nothing changed, and Caliban could never
wear a Hermes tie, or broker deals,
or throw his thunderbolts into heaven.

She'd sent him to the college chapel like Moses
upon the Nile, to Nefertiti's mercy:
but Our Lady of the Bloodless Roses
sought the weak, like the dominatrix Circe.

It only looked sybaritic from the outside
to the movie-themed three-act Creole vision –
confusing sacrifice with suicide.
The new curriculum had a single mission:

To enslave the free; to kill the spurts of life
that split the placid face of the black water;
to transform science into a crude knife
to pare the human bark of shoots of laughter.

But Jude could only yearn to be a captive
of the disciplined lines of the quadrangle
as he burned in the pit of the Senior Comprehensive,
the other college, where dreams were slowly strangled.

He took me inside that other place, and showed me
paseos of artless graffiti, the burnt-out cores
of classrooms, chalkboards whose fresh faces glowed
invitingly, but were marked only by the claws

Of the Creole girls, who sashayed through the halls
with hips and flouncy curls, like Ola, Michael's girl
in *Thriller*, who thrilled me sometimes with their catcalls,
showing me their sweet cunts, where heaven swirled.

V

In that strange moment when Timothy Dalton played
at Bond, before Pierce Brosnan made it his meat,
our manhood took us by surprise; it waylaid
us one night on a surly, deserted street;

We would roam sometimes through the back roads,
stop by the football field to watch the dark
energy spend itself till the choir of toads
intoned the day's last rites and the final spark

Was doused, then amble slowly through the town's heart
eyeing our reflections in the spiteful glass:
a gangly knight and a stocky friar, the start
of a picaresque fable; and *here* our moment passed

With a molten slowness; a broad-winged spiral that swallowed
childhood and left the future, for an instant, clear.
My devotion to Our Lady of the Hallowed
Quod had been found wanting, and Jude had fared

Badly in the college's Chapel Perilous.
The Grail he'd sought via the fawning short cut
was a mirage; he'd been dismissed with a querulous
benediction: *Your piety has bought*

Comfort for the souls suppurating in Limbo,
your name is written in the Book of Life.
And his earthly fate was written in play-dough,
a morbid tale of social and racial strife

And ugliness, which hardened suddenly,
in the brown concrete cells of the Main Road
that night, when shop doors and air hung leadenly,
the noisy flood of listless bodies slowed,

The mannequins in the windows wearing polyester
stared sardonically through their blotchy glass
at the sad storefronts, where time and desire festered
in musty haberdashery, mottled brass

And the empty eyes of the tea-skinned store girls.
As we walked past, he said: "Wait now and look
at them, they just like cage-up little squirrels.
Them never had a chance. And the old crook

Who cage them, in there too, till all of them dead.
This place too damn evil." But we had always
known it, had always felt the latent dread
of what writhed below the boredom: *the Malaise*,

Whose cure we'd found in panoramas of glowing
cityscapes where beauty walked with virtue
in six-inch heels, with hope always following;
where villains might, for effect, be allowed to hurt you

But in the end, you were saved by divine structure:
the standard, three-act symmetrical plot arc,
or a tinny Hollywood deus ex machina.
We could not conceive of our lives in the dark;

There was only the shining electric centre of light,
our burning bush, our plotted deliverance,
where streets spread wide, the buses blue and white,
and always on time, and our reasonable plans –

Of school, success, wingtips and two-button
grey department-store suits, with the counterpoint ties,
and houses, set against backdrops of cottony
clouds, in the omnipotent, boreal skies –

Glided, leaflike, into an open hand.
I sighed as his plane ascended a few months later;
America swallowed him, like a body in quicksand,
and let him be reborn, as his own creator.

YEARNING FOR THE CITY

(for Gerard Hutchinson)

It had been a yearning of his heart to find something to anchor to, to cling to; for some place which he could call admirable; should he find that place in this city if he could get there?
— Thomas Hardy

The bus's hydraulics hissed in the inky dark,
and set me down on an anonymous street
near a cobblestone square, lined with tram tracks
sentried by trees, their foliage forbidding
at 4 a.m., outside small, seedy hotels
whose pale-lit reception desks and solitary
wraithlike clerks I passed by, weary, tense,
to wait for morning in an all-night café.

And this was Antwerp as I met it – brooding,
a dark crystal of my longing for cities.

You know this dream: the burning for places of light;
Spenser saw a distant crystal city;
Hardy saw an anchor to transcendence,
a doctrine of eternity sculpted
from the granite of medieval mortification –
rococo creeds of earthly paradise.

My vision, time, the underside of my tongue
congealed in the two hours before the dawn
could come; I sat at a surly Formica table
absently tracing stains and sharp-rimmed cracks
into shapes of lifetimes unreal to me,
sketching the transient patterns of the real.
Nondescript people sat alone, smoking
and eating flaccid sandwiches; I felt
I had interrupted a millennium;
the security of books and myth was gone –
Dante, Spenser, Milton – nothing would rhyme
with any line that had come before.
The journey into darkness had begun from light
in another city – the familiar relief
whose dawn departure raises in the pilgrim
as he sits, fitted tightly into the body
of the behemoth bus, lumbering through

England's narrow ways and towns, finally
descending through new, bone-white vaulted archways,
winding down below the sea and sitting
patiently on the platform as the serpentine
train's body sloughed the tunnel's soft darkness
on to Europe's first outpost, at Calais,
and then through France's eerie night, along spectral
orange-limned highways. I remember silos
that loomed like monoliths on verdigris fields
which remembered echoes of giants facing down
the sharpened staves of vassal army lines
as their lords thundered past on screaming horses
beneath a rage of pennants and blood-red crosses.

We stopped at a gas station store at midnight,
about thirty of us, red-eyed, irritable,
willing the sickening scent of fertilizer,
the shelves of orange and green plastic packs,
mummified cakes and moribund chocolate,
into a fable to fade with the morning.
I bought a bottle of water, but the dream,
the sterilized eeriness, the chemical scent
undid even that reliable purity –
The human absolutes of thirst and water –
and we trudged back into the bus, suspended
between the Dantean ironies of unquenchable
desire, and the body's inexorable drive
to dissolve, finally, into soft sleep,
and enter the dream that all travellers share:
voluptuous beds; quiet, large-roomed hotels.

The dawn came slowly, searing the patina
of novelty. I saw myself in a mirror –
unhealthy, brown, raw eyes, a bloated face –
and looked away, into the multiplied sun
in the glass panels across the square. The trams

had just begun to rumble in, whining
where the tracks curved into the depot, and bodies
in sombre suits with featureless faces waited,
mingled with denim jackets, khaki slacks,
relentlessly straight dark hair; and beyond,
the city assembled its perspective from
the jumbled lines of sunlight, steel, and asphalt.

The university was silent, bland,
and closed, indifferent to my expectations;
the campus wove into the quiet back streets
of the business district, subdued in the sullen grey
of brokers, accountants, mediocre lawyers –
prosaic, paralysing. I don't know what
I expected: ivy-covered dark-brick walls,
transom windows exhaling heavy clouds
from smoky studies where severe men with goatees
and worsted wool suits argued and drank brandy –
I'm thinking of Freud and the Vienna Circle –
but that is how alien Antwerp was to me:
I was off by a century, and a nation.
The closest I could feel was Kurtz's Belgium,
ominous, grey, its sidewalks impossibly distant
from the damask-curtained sitting rooms
where ivory-skinned maidens imagined away
the dooms of their Beloveds' stolen kingdoms,
unmindful of the centuries that would drive
their doppelgangers to the heart of light
to brightness that slows our old disease of desire:
the fright in the tired eyes, the hesitancy
in the voice asking for directions, the paradox
of rage and desire so docile at indifference.

My host, Bénédicte, a youngish professor,
was my photo-positive – so pale
and cool, a new agent of the old enterprise –

she asked me if I'd slept, while writing me
into a corporeal plastic name-tag,
and offered me her room to rest awhile.
I toyed with her sliver of humanity
while wandering the fluorescent-lit corridors
seeking my convocation, looking in
on small congregations idly stroking
their pastel-coloured theories of the profound
throb of bongos and blood, while calculating
the value in Euro per diems.
My panel met in a small amphitheatre;
a solemn trio of auditors sat, solemnising
the black professor's beatification of
the Negro Titan, Eric Williams, while thinking
of Hakagawa among the Titians.
The quiet contempt echoed as I descended
into my own fugue, and at the end
I faded, thankfully, to Bénédicte's room.

It was late September; the early brightness retreated
into a prescient gloom that coloured my sleep
and I woke early, irrational, afraid
the bus would come and go, and leave me there,
where mere hours were enough to unmoor
the body from its dreams of transcendence.
I marvelled at my new fragility
as I sat, waiting for Bénédicte, looking
into the evening, down onto a narrow
anonymous back street. Then they appeared:
a riot of fleece, denim, straw-blonde hair,
Nike, Adidas, Levis; and, half-dreaming,
my first fleeting impression was of Elysian
beasts in search of their hyperborean shepherd.
They glided past in phalanx — swift, unmindful
of my intrusion in their millennium.
I envied them their light and swiftness, and thought

them beautiful, as natural in grey streets
as reindeer on tundra, heroes in history –
as history blends with its ideal in myth,
and clarifies the shapeless, shadowy yearning
into a single exhalation: *wholeness*:
a sense of belonging as effortless as peasants
sitting in the city's midnight cafés –
teenagers trooping through anonymous
side streets, bearing down on eternity,
enrapt in history, beauty, and without fear.

Early evening, and another café
in a small piazza with pink, bow-tied waiters
and a carafe of wine; to the side a movie-
theatre. I cannot see the dingy café
where I met the morning. After sleep
and food, calm, relaxed, I see a different
city – the unassuming office towers,
the self-assured vernacular buildings,
the lapidary high-ceilinged steel and glass
of the Metro station – it is more than modern;
it is millennial, an eternal present,
and I hover, outside of time, watching it spin.

Outside of time, but I still feared it. I sat
across from the street where the bus would come
at midnight, for three hours – an hour after
the café closed. I finished my wine and took
a final breath from my apogee, and was
shown the vision to complete my epoch:
The Beloved, arm in arm with her Intended
in the square – his ivory teeth, the gravity
of his black face in the soft blue evening
threading history through her flaxen hair

Meanwhile, on the other arm of the square

37

another chamber of the city's mind
opened, as I watched, ghostlike, my hand
encircling my ticket like a talisman,
the cars sliding through the dark, disgorging
Muslim women in burkas, Chinese men
in too-new clothes, sunglasses and baseball caps,
African women in bright dresses and braids
tending old Arab women, and Syrian merchants
in rumpled brown suits with open-necked
shirts and gold medallions nesting in ursine
chest-hair. I happily thought of Dante then,
and the bus as Charon's boat, conveyance of
the perplexedly dead to their waiting horrors,
and when it did arrive, a half-hour early
as I had feared, it brought with it *Marat-Sade*:
the driver and conductor could have stepped
from the Brothers Grimm: a balding chinless man
who never looked away from the windscreen
and an ugly, hostile dwarf with jagged teeth –
his wife, and conductor – who barked at us as if
this were another century, our passage
another enterprise, and they, the grotesque
dyad, were miniature panjandrums
conducting trains of slaves through Empire's
subtle vessels, the fuel of subterranean
engines that enraged their Enlightenment.
I saw it, and so did the company:
the Arab women lumbering docilely
followed by their glowering African maids,
and then the Chinese, Syrians, Muslims, and me,
finally, rediscovering irony.

The Grimms at first pretended not to hear
the questions as they bypassed the rest stops,
and finally, the dwarf addressed the cursing,
screaming congregation, muttering threats

about summoning police; and so it went
for hours until Calais, and the company
emerged, sick, enraged, into the accusatory
stares of the satraps that command the transits
between heaven, earth and hell – the bureaucrats.
My journey was near its end, but the company,
the Arab grandmothers, their Nubian Slaves,
the Chinese, Syrians, were entering
another ring. In the funereal queue
the fleshy lips constricted, and jaws tensed
and practised eyes were drawn inexorably
past the desks to the warren of white-walled cells
where the inquisition of pilgrims' faiths
and lives convened, and judged the travellers,
deciding fates, indifferent to the assurances
of the lesser Gods of travellers whose edicts,
spoken in foreign tongues, meant nothing here.
My fate was evident from my empty eyes.
They peered in and dismissed me back to the bus,
and my dream ended there, on the tunnel's edge
as I waited to re-enter the old life –
the island that lived in the eternal past.
But then, having travelled beyond the sun
the story of my truer life had begun.

TORONTO

(For D.A. Trotz)

He'd taken to roving the city, aimlessly, waiting for a coincidence.
None came.

                         – Thomas Pynchon

I

The malls are bright and empty before noon.
Stricken bodies in electric chairs whirr through
the corridors at Yorkdale, toward the cocoon

of the food court, to park and gape at the blue
beyond the skylight, enrapt in a single thesis:
transubstantiation: could it be true?

Can the body be shed, as the soul passes
through the labyrinth of its earthly seat?
The same mystery haunts the coloured masses

elsewhere under the mullioned sky – the defeat
of coal-faced gods by linear time, and space
that entombs them in bodies of sand and heat.

And I see them, somehow, in this sprawling place
where, like a refugee from a forgotten war,
I drag our history seeking a canon of Grace

Through stolid intersections that echo the core
of the void woven into its name: *Toronto*
and the dray gouges the path from an ancient door

Marked *The Fortunate* – now too far gone to
even see except through cowardly nostalgia
for the place the newly reborn cannot return to:

The Past. And it is this Future, as indulgence
for the sins of envy, dissatisfaction and lust,
(to say nothing of the other, vulgar

Pangs of the flesh, and the moist thighs of the dust)
that lures us, and me, into these places of light,
stations where History's rages and its curse

Can be soothed by a yearly sheath of white
amnesia which smoothens grotesqueries round
and banishes the terror of natural night,

As bright and dark succumb to the HD sound
of *that which is to come*: through a golden arch
a Saviour, and salvation, will come down –

Just not today. So the Newcomers' trundling march
continues through the broad downtown streets,
along schizophrenic avenues that ratchet

From the glassy baroque of Yonge and Bloor to feats
of pioneer will, down Dufferin, in Victorian
raw brick tenements hemmed in by pleats

Of tram tracks, which drive the phantasmagoria
of tribes still trapped in native dreams, & whose curse
is that they cannot be stitched into one story and

Moral – of sheep, or loaves – or a single thirst
that a pure fluid, or simple Truth, will slake.
And so the relentless journey: to immerse

In the glowering waters of the narcotic lake
to dissolve the stains of Originary Sin,
and emerge from darkness into electric daybreak.

But it doesn't work that way, and the garden
by the lake shore is called Gethsemane,
Disney's gory remake of Classical Eden.

II

So, escape, flight, desire for a New World –
the malaise of ambition, the ancient vice
whose delirium drove *shudras* to hurl

Their lives into black waters, shrugging off cries
of Brahmin *kathas* extolling the karmic dirt,
to escape Samsara, to earthly paradise

Without the tiresome labour of endless rebirth.
That was my early inheritance: a sweet
kingdom carved from a newly imagined Earth.

But, as in the epics, victory seeds defeat
and the sweet Republic did not survive its freedom;
the peasants began to pine for Brahmins' feet

And cultivate rococo memories of their serfdom –
not from the Epics or Sages, but through the haze
of the Bollywood diorama, whose songs had become

Garlands for the many-limbed gods they worshipped in ways
that flattened grimy impastos of peasant strife
into pastels of luminous, cane-scented days.

And there, midway through the promised life
I found myself staring into evil's
caramel-eyed, smooth-cheeked face, in a time rife

With tired sighs of fear and the grind of tumbrels
of ideas and innocents – from the muddy plains
and seething favelas on lacerated hills

To set the blank-eyed detritus on Port of Spain's
slanted streets and leave them there to rot,
to stain the flowery friezes, clog the drains,

And splay their foetid memories to blot
the slate-grey faces of the Hall of Justice.
All this, and more, I could live with, but not

The sickness that cupped the bled-out face in crisis
to paint a masque on it, and design costumes
to reshape the racked, contorted limbs, to disguise

Inherited pain with dyes and ostrich plumes,
and call its metal-tongued music of suffering
songs of hope. Such delusion consumes

Without the softness that only irony can bring
to the stony faith in the literal word
that leaves the sign entrapped in the single thing,

And drives the civilization into the Absurd.
The Absurd – where meaning has no fixity
and sheep and goat alike are put to the sword,

Where fleshy, spittle-flecked charlatans evoke pity
but Nanking and Dachau are good for helpless laughter
and sages can only sigh: *Hell is a city*

Much like Port of Spain, and only the hereafter
offers grace and hope to the minor sinner –
the liar, thief, *the charlatan with a daughter*.

I named her after a Goddess of Light: *Aurora*,
and as much as I could bear my sugary vale
of drear, only the sky would do for her.

Thus the old malaise made new again: a Grail
legend, with its own mythology: Salvation
by immigration, and priced for easy sale.

The old hook remained – escaping damnation –
but the sermons changed. The vague eternal bliss
became *free health-care, safety, education,*

A country for raising children, an oasis
consistently rated the best place to live.
But first the money, then the screening process

And then, like the white light the dying strive
to reach, the fortunate, after years of hope
are shown the door and told they have arrived.

III

I landed in a throng – like pilgrims or convicts,
I thought, as my fore-peasants had come, from the mists
of grime – wearily dragging my bundle of tricks,

My Baedeker, *The Comedy*; my Virgil, Alissa,
a dark-haired Valkyrie the Fates assigned
to guide me through the city's cryptic twists,

Its grey venation of streets, its turbid mind,
its skyscraper vaults that housed my Grail: *sentience.*
I felt somehow she had always divined

My undoing: *the Harpies*, waiting with practised patience
on help-line phones the wretched call to ask:
But where is the sun? – though she hid her prescience,

Shepherding me through each Sisyphean task
while murmuring from the missal of Guyanese wisdom:
"I don't know how you stand these fockin' ass,

Nuh. You and me blasted husband. Two of you come
here smiling and feel these blasted people like you.
Eh heh." And in truth, the more I saw of the kingdom —

Its feuilleton rage for the blue-eyed and new,
its spidery side-streets tracing ancient gyres,
the tinny smiles from the bureaucrat revue

That receives complaints, and occasionally inquires:
Why are the niggers bawling? Then issues a grim
edict about *Newcomers Canada Desperately Requires*

Then returns to sleep — the more the white light dimmed.
And in the softer light, the subtler lines
of the city's architecture appeared to limn

Another pathway, more intricately designed,
to guide the coarser granules through its skin,
the grist for its bowels' multi-culti grind.

And, resignedly, I sighed and was sucked in
to the spiral-ceilinged skein of the uncanny,
to trudge, again, into another beginning.

The other city behind the soignée marquee
was, I suppose, no surprise, or heaven —
it is the grimace in shadow we cannot see

That speaks most plainly; and here, façade riven,
I crossed the threshold into its quotidian life:
the streetcars, supermarkets, the logic woven

Into the bevelled smiles of shop clerks, the stifled
rage of poets and scientists whose nostrums
of orderly algorithms and metred strife

Nurtured in distant Oriental kingdoms
where mysticism defeated logic, dreams
were fate, and hope was swallowed by koan-like chasms

Now dissolved in the baptismal wash of memes
that re-inscribed pioneer fantasias,
and harden Duchenne curves into seams

Of quiet anger, contorted in embrasures
of corrugated brows and noose-knotted ties,
helpless before the spectacular erasures

Of mendhis, henna-streaked hair, the ritual lies
of monkey-headed gods, their money, and hopes,
encased in lonely taxicab cages and wet eyes

That go dim as first the fingers, then memory gropes
at formulae, scalpels, vital strings to unravel
the tapestry, unhook the rigging ropes

Of this initial conflict – the judge's gavel
of courtroom drama that brings the opening act
to a scheduled tightening of the gut, and gravel

To the throat, and tears, and then fades to black,
then the slow, inexorable rappel to freedom,
all accompanied by the appropriate soundtrack.

IV

I brushed their degrading orbits drifting from
the interviews and the job clubs, the coaches
and bread-crumb mills, that peddle the omnibus nostrum

Of the future waiting for determined searchers
with sharpened résumés, and English skills –
the script is everywhere, in the malls, churches,

On the split lips of dried-out, broken wills
which repeat it, endlessly, like a Tibetan prayer wheel.
I saw it at the agencies, how the mills

Strip the fragile striae of hope and anneal
the tendrils of doubt into a muscular fear
that gives the counsellors' rehearsed smiles the feel

Of death under the life that called them here
as they gleefully send science and art to network
with wraiths and Walmart spotters at the job fair.

Thus sculpted, I trailed my crumbs to the North York
Civic Centre, one surly wool-grey evening,
disguised – suited and ritually perked –

I slid like an unschooled shark beneath the grieving
November sky, up terraced steps, to a tomb
with folding tables, Bristol-board signs weaving

The composed faces behind each paper loom,
inviting name-tags, silky verbal caresses,
a falling refrain: *consume or be consumed*.

The Asian lady with the face of a goddess
sitting serenely in a Buddhist temple, smiled
and sang to me – it sounded like she blessed

Me with an ancient prayer, in English – beguiling,
the creamy lilt that floated the protean "Product";
I could become rich selling, the lifestyle

I could have: "You are so handsome, I see luck
in your face…" The tenderness startled me, the words,
her trembling lips, her nervous fingers, the fucked-up

World that smirks at good and evil and herds
the innocent with the vile on Charon's sleigh.
But her voice was like a feast of crimson birds

And I smiled and listened, lingered around the display
until the pantomime played out, and the bows
taken, and her card pocketed, I turned away

Into Shobhi's streaked brown hair, her upturned nose
and knowing smile. I exuded promise; she saw
it in the suit, not like the others, those

Who were so *plainly* out of depth and flawed.
*My company sends me to these things on the chance
of ones like you*. The hairs on her silky paw

Grazed my palm, and I felt her practised hands
in my hair as I licked her syrupy pussy: "*Yeah* –"
And palmed her card as the Spirit broke the trance.

She'd appeared as I entered, and hovered near,
parsing the prospects in my conversations,
but the practised Oreads sensed the spoor of fear

And kept her at bay – the nervy, thick vibrations
from the gibbous face, the darting, teal-blue eyes,
the head-tie, the men's workboots – intimations

Of the Circle of the Alone and Un-realised.
She trailed me to the unhappy, sallow Indian
selling insurance. He gauged me, unsurprised

At my accent. He knew opportunities had thinned and
was sure I was more than I seemed. He offered a reprieve,
his proven system: "It's not a job; you can find an

Incredible life." I was tired, ready to leave.
I nodded and turned away, and he said: "Your number."
I mumbled a few digits, which he perceived

Were false. As his lips pursed, I'd already wandered
to another booth, and then another, until
she flagged. And suddenly, I yearned for the sombre

Evening outside, and weary with failure, cavilled
into desperation, I stumbled out.
She sat alone, tragic, in the concrete sill

Of a bay window, peering into the mouth
of the bristling dusk. It occurred to me then:
my journey was over. But the dewy snout

Of defeat taunted me, and I turned to spend
the last vapours of hope I'd breathed these months
and stared into her reflection: "The Caribbean?

That's where you're from?" She smiled, and all at once
the body came to life, the fingers, thick and wrinkled,
flexed, the yellow face glowed, and the sparkling ponds

Opened. "Oh, you are like me. I didn't think, well,
I thought, you know, of India, but your voice
is good to hear." The Jamaican bells still tinkled.

Her delightful name was Artress. Its boldness hoisted
me out of my pity and I smiled and listened
to her story, glad to drown my own tired noise.

"It's my real name, you know, how I was christened
in Jamaica. I've been here for years and years, oh, since
the '70s. That's so long, I don't even miss them

Any more, my family. You know, the world spins
around whether you pay attention or not.
and I've always worked, you know, I have done stints

As a waitress, secretary, I've always thought
it best to do what you can, but the accident
changed things. I slipped on a bus, and I was caught

In the door, dragged a little way. They sent
me to therapy, and gave me money, and I
was fine. But the injury, you know, it meant

I couldn't do certain jobs. I thought I'd try
to stay at home, but it was so lonely; I had
to do something. My aspirations weren't high,

I just wanted to work. I would be glad
just being with people. I worked as a secretary
in a big firm, but the hours sitting were bad

For my back; I had to leave. They were very
sad to see me go, they said, and gave
me such nice references, I was so sorry

To leave them but you have to turn and wave
goodbye sometimes. It's sad, no matter what
you do, it all goes away, and you have to be brave…"

I smiled at her and felt my fears welling, hot
and slow. In the hollows between the words a sleek
slash of emptiness raced, the ghost of thought

She'd lost, and my rankling doubts began to speak:
*Would I forget Aurora? Would all I'd brought
fade so quickly, and leave a world so bleak*

*All I had to remain alive was the thought
of work, and haunting the weary?* Somewhere between
her discovery of Everest College, the final port

Of crawl for the forlornly unskilled to glean
the low-hanging fruits of the new economy,
her story began to falter, the hopeful sheen

Of honest sweat faded, and they fell from me –
hope, and irony. My grip on the comedy
loosed, and my dreams crumbled in ignominy.

The fantasy to escape the past – the sum of the
confinements in barracoons of chance and birth;
the peasant's ancient desire to hear the hum in the

Valley tops, to leave the foothill dirt
and touch the lightest music – of his daughter
laughing, singing in a rising concert

With the future – transformed to pleas trailing after
a stranger, in a temple of futility
where dreams, like sloe-eyed lambs, gather for slaughter.

V

I lived in a warren of cells on Dundas West
let by a Chinese woman, who scratched the rent
receipts in a Chinatown optometrist's

Memo pad. The inscrutable Hanzi blent
contemptuously with the sinuous dollar signs
that traced the cost of every moment I dreamt –

Idly sketching now solid, now hazy outlines
of a black-roofed gabled house with airy rooms,
red-lidded oculi, sclera of icy blinds;

Riding the streetcars down College, scrying plumes
that braised the mouths of the red-brick chimneys;
imagining the lives in blue-curtained bedrooms

Sitting morosely on seedy storefronts, or primly
in Victorian houses – memorizing then forgetting
the damp/dry lines of fence palings; the grim trees

With skeletal limbs in Dufferin Grove; the unsettling
sepulchral glyph of the electric wheelchair
gliding over a snow-lathered sidewalk; the carets in

Vowels of the French street signs in Kensington where,
ensphered with the hipsters in Navy surplus
pea coats, and toques that spilled unruly hair

Onto angelic faces and eyes engrossed
in a shining city I couldn't see. I reached
again and again for it – the susurrus

Of hope, the movie-plot future, the snowy beach
that yearned for my footprint, the tide of simony
I'd sailed here on, even the mushy speeches

At the job fair, and inexorably, the sunny
terror of gold-streaked hair, the houri smile,
and with the comedy gone, I steamrolled irony

And called her. I felt like Moses on the Nile
drifting along Queen Street that morning, walking
to her office. Her velvety fingers stroked my file

And her lips glistened a little as we talked,
but the script was wooden; she was only the lure
they dangled; inside waited the snowy hawk –

Grey hair, a good suit, and a smile to reassure
me. "You know, you're the type we talk about,
Shobhi told me. This is not a guy we should ignore."

The daydream flooded the room, but a germ of doubt
winked at me and drilled into my gut;
fed by the spiel, cilia began to sprout –

"…a partnership; we work *with* you, then put
you at the right door, with a name, a *brand*
you *become*…" I waited for the cut,

The moment he'd stop incanting and spit the sand
in my eyes. The office sat square and grey. The art
on the wall was the window. "…our manager, Shobhi's husband…"

I thought of her in stilettos, legs apart,
orchid-purple lips, with me between
and kissing her, tenderly, listening for her heart.

"So what do you think? An arrangement with us would mean
an entrée into places you wouldn't know
were there, and open to you. Now that you've seen

What we have to offer, how far it's possible to go…"
And what, I marvelled, would the journey cost?
He smiled, and at last, flashed the steel below.

"Of course, you have a credit card?" *Of course.*
The dream had blunted the iron edge of the world –
its engines, its glassed-in cities built on the dross

Of dreamers, charlatans, minor sinners, moulded
into its pillars with their dreams, and their daughters.
"It's very tempting," I said, and the moment unfurled.

I grimaced at the other fish from the waters
of the narcotic lake, and slipped by their eyes
through the anteroom where they sat, like expectant courtiers.

The buildings' faces, daubed with cold-creamy skies
that swathed the city, waited impassively outside.
The wind sliced through the glassy canyon, and sighed

A little, in satisfaction, like a neap tide
kept only by chance from a hidden bay,
released by nature, finally raging inside.

VI

There was one place I could shed the disguise,
and where I went sometimes to inveigle fate
and glower at the thing I most despised –

In truth, myself, in another eigenstate,
floating through the Scarborough Town Centre
free of body, history, and dolorous weight.

The city's soaring life begins its descent here.
Black and brown and off-white bodies amble
through marble corridors, each bearing an accent —

A history, future, or dream the city had humbled
and shown its allotted place: *the margins*, a bulwark
against the sharp-edged silences that tumble

Down the glaciers, through the prairies, a stark
limit, beyond which crackles the coronal mind
of the Guyanese girl with the pink voice and dark

Skin, in knee-high boots and fake-fur lined
coat, or the roaring dreams of Jamaican gold-toothed
strays around McDonald's, or the rind

Of Russian, Bajan, Tamil sonorities smoothed
in the city's churning bowels. Looking at them
I thought of insects swarming a burnt-out crude

Log, seeking the node from which a green stem
might sprout — the parents in the food-court, ashy, small,
yet content, who carried with them all they'd become,

From the Haitian hut or Georgian gulag they'd crawled
from — tear-stained paths their children could never know.
And *that story* — the muddy foot in the marble hall,

The splintered dreams, were the only seeds that would grow
in concrete soil. It was the only trope
the bluest eye would ever see, its own glow

Enlightening the darker races with hope
of a pure golden imago from mongrel brass,
and the parable of patience before the slope

Of the city's pyramid of steel and glass
inside of which the promised future gleamed,
incalculably. More detail would be crass,

Might harden ambition, and then redemption might seem
to be something else, a state that was *unequal* –
and what is a Redeemer without the Redeemed?

And what about taxi drivers, exotic clerks in the mall?
What about the pain, for our imago to feed?
What about the turbine, which might finally stall

If the tide of those dark bodies would recede?
And there, on the margins, the chaos fed the fear;
the masses refused to mutter a single creed;

In the myriad dialects, each would only hear
his own, and stubbornly cling to an old pain
the way a child ignores the stars to stare

At the dark corner of his room, where a stain
becomes a hieroglyph – a vital icon
of a secret world that he alone can explain,

A geography enacted under a fading sun
on a creased tourist poster in a Scarborough basement,
where plastic palms and sawdust wait to be spun

Into gold on old turntables by surly-faced men
who, by day, are mahouts for the behemoth streetcars,
whose callused hands build and bolt the emplacement

Of the virtual to its concrete body, the centaurs
who link the city's haloes and iron cores,
but who, by night, peel off quotidian scars,

Exhaling memory into calypso scores
that breathe life and heat into the plastic palms,
and spread the unseen white breakers into gauze

That salves the riotous memories, and calms
the roiling dreams of loss and exile to gentle
nostalgia, which comforts as it embalms

The affection for tribal scars, the iron mental
manacles and chokers they now wear by choice,
the trifles of history thus made incidental.

Their weight and presence stilled the perpetual noise
of promised futures, and at last I heard it move:
The human machinery, seeking equipoise.

In all my time here I had not thought of love
nor heard it spoken, nor saw it bloom or grow,
and I'd never seen the city from above.

I'd believed somehow that below the frost and snow
existed a life I could someday slip into,
and lose myself in a joyous anonymous flow.

But I lacked my fore-peasants' gifts to plant and hew
a life out of alien, unforgiving earth,
to abandon all that I had made and knew –

My daughter, my dreams, made precious by the dirt
that anchored them. And I finally caressed my fears;
my fate was not the sea, it was the desert.

VII

The taxi's thick haunches and aquiline head
hardened from the five a.m murk. I waited
in a mush of snow and tobacco, my eyes red,

Mouth dry. I had not slept, the Furies not sated
by dreams of rain, no matter how sweet or warm.
The taxi sank a little at the suitcases' weight,

And I, now lighter, sank into the calm
as the car sluiced through the grey asphalt river,
then through pools of orange light, then embalmed

Again by the slate-dark. The African driver
listened to the BBC, and flicked
his eyes into the mirror at each sliver

Of chaos from outside – Mubarak's Egypt,
spontaneous uprisings in Yemen, Tunisia –
nodding as if he'd been vindicated. I slipped

In and out of the moment. Was it easier
to be here when the explosion came, unmarked
and safe, and empty; or there – bloody, messier

And empty. *Empty*. Then opened my eyes to dark,
the taxi, glassed-round towers looming beyond
the futile sodium suns, and there, a spark;

Through sliding doors, a *glowing blue screen*, a beacon
taunting deserters and calling the in-rolling waves
from the stormy places – not a marquee in neon;

A palimpsest, an unspoken promise to slaves:
The future must be written. Or it could have been
a television left on; failure craves

A reason, even one resembling a dream.
The night soon dissolved into an acidic
morning – silvery, glowering, eroding the theme

From despair to resignation, with sporadic
anger smashing windows as I smiled wanly
with the bright agent, ignoring the soporific

Heat in the terminal, blurring my eyes as I scanned the
surreal blend of hopeful eyes, crumpled coats,
anonymity. I sat, staring blandly

At the departure board, then at the berths
where jets sat, tethered by long aluminium straws
which siphoned votive bodies into their throats,

I thought, and bristled a little at the claws
of metaphor which, I knew, would be useless
once I stepped through the automatic doors.

THE DREAM DIARY

December, 2005

And in truth, you appeared from the sky —
an inspired moment: a satori

made of the things of two decades,
of fights and lust and love-forged blades

that shave away the dross that builds
stony mountains from silly molehills.

Your mother described such thrilling deeds
as "seeing to your father's needs"

and kept you to herself for months;
she said she'd been frightened into silence.

And when the doctors were finally called
they, and I, were less than enthralled,

and there were tests, and waiting, and fear
of obstructions in your passage here,

and fear slowed time's surge to a trickle
that made the first months chimerical.

Your mother became melancholy,
and I ploughed the freezing sea of folly,

navigating the shoals of genetics
and monsters of medical statistics,

but by the fourth month, when we knew
that if we wanted we could keep you,

the cold humours began to warm
and I could look at the sonogram

and begin to know you, if in outline —
the throbbing heart, the supple spine,

the curious hands that reached at things,
the little lungs that fluttered like wings.

Is it macabre to tell you this,
that we tested your perfectness?

Of the emptiness that would have been
if we'd given you a darkling gene?

January, 2006

It wakes me sometimes in the night
in a paralysing, primal fright —

the beast that lurks at sleep's border —
and I reach across and touch your mother

for the safety of the curve you sleep in
and then my shallow breaths deepen.

I dream of ordinary things,
of monkey bars and playground swings

and the little bodies that make them go
and the plain parents who watch them grow,

and a strange absence invades my dreams
and I know, I know how small it seems —

the anxiety over the ordinary;
it's so annoying, so contrary

to everything you'd expect of us
who look down upon the breeding classes.

But it's there, and nothing I can say
can send the red-eyed beast away;

and you cannot know the anguish, pretty,
of distant probability.

Your parents' lives have been undone
for so little reason, and so often

by the mindless toil of patient drones
who boasted their hearts were bloodless stones,

and then you came to us from the sky,
a golden, hesitant butterfly,

floating fickly toward our hands,
appraising the world in wild wingspans.

February, 2006

The Sunday before Carnival:
we found out today that you're a girl

and... what to say, and how to say it,
in the confines of a four-foot couplet?

You might, as you read this years from now,
detect a tilt in the lines below,

a shift in register and stress,
a more delicate tone of address,

because I'd unconsciously begun
to make myself into you: a son.

And now all is soft and luminous
as I stumble through *terra nullius*

and look for the right language for you –
of me, but not me: something new.

Now I begin to understand God
and the deeper meaning of his blood,

and laugh at myself for thinking this way:
people have daughters every day.

But this is pure animal delight,
to glory in shadow, and forget the night,

enchantment at a swirling cape,
ignoring the lines of its darker shape,

to look at a single life unfurl
and believe it superordains the whole.

April, 2006

I'm looking at this spiralling world
and thinking about a little girl;

the fabric of the river is rent,
as the fury of hopeless lives is spent,

heaven's mooring chains are cut,
its rusting iron doors groan shut;

as the complement of saints returns
to heaven, the final indulgence burns.

Now for those awake enough to see
the choice is despair or fantasy.

Our last hope is bars or schism:
the world is either illusion or prison.

But this means that spiders and moonbeams –
all the things that wring girly screams

from safe inside your father's arms –
are mere plays of light and pixel charms;

but I don't want that world for you,
where everything dies to be new.

I want a world of teddy bears
and pink jewels like little tears,

to see your milky baby teeth
and plaster casts of your little feet.

I want to remember the three of us,
when my thumbs curl in and eyes glass,

your little face, all pink and sweet,
amidst life on some Toronto street,

walking through a perfect day
towards the end of a mild May.

May, 2006

Walcott could write about his gift at forty
in language unleavened by irony – a sortie
into the many-fountained courtyard of myth,
to touch the pedestal where his bust would sit.

Your father at thirty-eight can only see,
in his past, the yellow clay of parody;
his murmurs to nobility unheard,
his gestures at art pointing to the absurd.

Before you awoke, when he met the thought,
his cure was to reduce himself to nought;
in the eddies of opiate time he'd imagine
that his brief breath had simply never been.

But your golden life came, like a little bird,
whose song gave meaning to the tuneless absurd;
now he is startled at the sight of his best frown
from a mouth and nose no longer his alone,

On a little face as familiar as the Sphinx
whose grimaces, he is told, transmit instincts
it breathes from air he colours with his moods,
when he stares angrily at the rain and broods.

And yet clouds do not lift, nor the sun smile,
nor anything desert its accustomed style,
and no signposts appear to show the way,
nor any music keep the beasts at bay.

But now he can stop and look away from it all
to a life, with a garden from before the Fall,
and know its bowers and shady seat
will not postpone his eventual defeat.

There will be no bust or monument
for him; only these couplets and this moment.
For this is all your father can bequeath
before the yellow clay encrusts his feet.

November 2007

So now at forty, I sit at home at night
and watch romantic comedies
(while rolling phrases about dying light
and time's insatiable eddies)
which never tire of the humdrum happiness
of little people like your parents.
Your mother's and my body will never rest
together again, and our essences
will never twine as in your riotous hair,
or the harmony of your pink limbs.
She has been away from you for three months now
and has grieved for the primal hymns
of your first words that fill the world as you grow,
that are inscribed on our marriage bier.

January 2008

Here, at dusk, I think of pioneer
women in gingham dresses, and quite alone
on crude, log-walled homesteads on the frontier
of un-hewn America, staring down the unknown,
caressing the small faces of their children
as shrieking lassos of ancient fear draw nearer
on ponies, to take their men at a dead run,
with faces smeared in red and black and terror.

And I know that I can only protect you now,
here in my arms, under the green parrots'
screams as the trees swallow them for the night.
Even though there is still an hour of light,
already the power lines become garrotes,
closing in on our time as the shadows grow.

February 2008

This is something poetry cannot say:
the silence when a child is taken away.

March 2008

My most terrible torment was a dream where you sat
near a broken wall. Your face was stained.
I saw dark blood that ran in a small train
from your lips, and your eyes were dull and flat.
Then I awoke into another dream
and knowing I was dreaming I cried and cried,
"Look, look at what they've done to my child!"
But I knew even then it was useless to scream.
Now, inside a dream, I am in a room
in an hotel in the American mid-west,
with muted lights, a writing desk, a crest
with an otter on the stationery, and doom
sitting idly outside the brown oak door.
A few miles away, there sits a small
bench in the plaza of a bright-lit mall,
where a man can hide among the poor
in spirit, while his pursuers smoke cigars
and send their hawks to hunt in the grey night.
These dreams of anonymity and flight
are all I have left, like the refugees of wars

in countries we know by name alone – Sudan,
Rwanda – where the horror is muted by distance
from those resigned black faces and clawing hands,
and the seething evil in the sea of sand.

June 6, 2008

Some day, perhaps in a rail station somewhere,
your eye will meet itself in bleary glass
and, if you are like me, you will start and stare
into yourself, as you recognize the past
in disconnected scenes: a little girl
of two in another country, with her daddy
in a doctor's office. It is a different world;
the father is happy at the scene, and glad he
could be there in the moment as she struggles
to mount a wooden horse. He coaches her
until she tires, and sees a pair of goggles
and smoothly dismounts. But as she approaches,
another patient grabs them away – a boy
whose mother sits nearby with his screaming twin.
She is stunned, stares after the taken toy,
and at that moment becomes enmeshed in sin.
Her father watches silently, aware
that something golden in their lives has ended,
that the confusion in her face will clear
and the certainty of evil will wend in.
Now I, the father, worry about your journey
to the nameless station with the hazy glass;
and wonder where and how you will earn the
calm that pain must teach – the tests where to pass
is to fail, and bruises count as marks of beauty.
The world of the place outside the doctor's office
is so far from the world of ideas and truth

and so indifferent to your light and softness
that I offer this poem as a kind of prayer
for the nameless glass, for hands that will know you
and capture your glances, caress your hair
but never know the magic from which they grew.

August 10, 2008

I'm reading Milan Kundera's *Life is Elsewhere* —
his savaging of a poet named Jaromil —
in the strangest season of my life and the year;
a time, and book, that bring to a standstill
the rages of forty years — a fury and life
I'd believed were immune to irony: you,
and my love for you. The time is one of strife,
a time, the Jews believe, when blood is due
(the month of Av, a feast in the old temple
for Adonai from insensible lambs' slaughter),
while Kundera lingers on Jaromil's dimple
then murders him quietly to farcical laughter
and makes his poems just sad props to the joke.
And I wonder whether there will even be laughter
when my poems for you transform to smoke,
when the characters of man and daughter
are dispatched or erased by the impatient author
to disentangle this most artless plot,
where parents' sins create the child martyr.
I think this is why you scream at her, but not
your father, who you reach with willing hands,
as we relive an ancient monody
and twice a week flail in a macabre dance
of Solomonic court-ordered joint custody,
when your little heart must readjust its rhythm
too quickly to different lives and different rooms;
as indifferently as the stony-faced HaShem
directs poems, and love, to unlit tombs.

August 19, 2008

The movie, ironically, is called *Doomsday*;
the apartment is appropriately bare,
the furniture is gone but the red sofa stayed
with the creaky bed, my books, my desk and chair.
One memory of many of you here: standing
on the sofa next to the stationary bike
and smiling at the camera, with one hand in
your mother's, the other waving. But then, unlike
tonight, was our morning, and our themes were benign.
It's dark now, and the story apocalyptic,
of a ravaged future where hope is consigned
to ruins, and tattooed underfed proles pick
at the charred flesh of minor characters.
The heroine is a young dark-haired girl,
modelled in the mould of defiant malefactors,
whose mother gave her up at the end of the world
to a soldier, moments before hell began.
The irony is that she becomes a soldier
and is chosen to return to the wasteland,
where she conquers her inheritance of fear,
and chooses, dramatically, to stay there.
It is tiresome, I know, that I should see us
in even a pulpy movie plot (even where,
to fit, I must become Tiresias),
but tonight, I have arrived at an impasse.
The time is coming when I will have to choose
to leave you here or stay for the absurd last
act. Your mother is determined to lose
the game we made of our lives, and to use
you in the final twist of the threads that bound us
into a motherly, hand-woven noose
that everywhere now closes in around us.
If I leave you, a chance exists that you
will survive the tragedy of Trinidad,

and some day, soon, I can return and rescue
you from the ruins of the land of the mad.
But if I stay, and the gates close in on us,
we are locked in a B-movie where the proles
already eat enemies, ambition is lust,
and the price to keep our bodies is our souls –
it's an old plot with no possibility
for the young heroine, or poetic vengeance
in the tragic ruin of an ancient city.
No chance, even, of saving innocence.

October 25, 2008

It is a week before my forty-
first birthday, reading *Gravity's Rainbow* –
I've just put it down as Slothrop's caught on
a Nazi sound stage in a tableau
with a lost actress, Margherita Erdmann,
and a whip with a black lacquer
handle. You can guess what happened,
but not her last word – Bianca –
the name of her lost daughter, whimpered
as the camera panned to close the scene.
And with that, the familiar flood –
our fates, the plot, and what they mean.
I think you sense it; your moods these weeks
have been unnerving; tears from nothing,
and screams, and sometimes little streaks
of fright as you glimpse at what is coming,
like when I take you to the sea
and the waves playfully immerse
you for a moment. Divided we
only stare at each other, helpless
in a glassy voix céleste. The moment

freezes, and seems to want to grow,
and though I reach you in an instant,
your shivering body seems to echo
what is coming, in the world
and in the book. The fate of the child
is a kind of darkness a father's soul
should never know, a kind of bile
that kills the earth we tread upon.
I fear the future that I see;
where we drift, separate, alone,
taunted by an artless ennui.

Nov 1, 2008

We started off beneath a surly sky
we two alone;
you stayed asleep most of the way, but I
saw tenderness looking
back in the mirror; you slept through flooded roads,
and past the pillars;
in Santa Cruz you missed the stranded toads
sitting forlornly
beside mudslides, surveying splintered trees
cracking the snaking
asphalt skin, and blinking as the car wheezed
up through the hills.
I romanticized randomness, as I
am wont to do;
the car became a refuge, warm and dry
against a storm
whose spidery wet fingers traced our steps;
and always ahead
the clouds dissolved into grey, fraying wefts
as the effortless blue

brightened the future we were driving to,
and it seemed, somehow,
that the metaphor had spun absurdly true.
The rain receded
before the car, and as we turned the final
gleaming corner,
the asphalt suddenly faded to a virginal
dryness, and the sea
sparkled behind the apron of spongy sand.
We sat on a log
and watched the pink purity your parents
had drawn from love
soothe the sloshy seas and the angry currents
to a placid silence
that studied our footprints' asymmetry
inconclusively
as the waves erased them, like an old country
pilgrims forget.
Driving back, I thought about the future
we hurtled towards,
and fantasized the journey as something pure:
an enigmatic
unfolding, the irony of starting in gloom
and ending in light,
somehow, somehow just evading doom.
Then at the end,
as I was leaving to go, emptied by fight,
you said to me
at the door: "Daddy, you stay here the night."
Your first sentence,
which showed a life that moved by its own volition.
You might forget
the moment, but for me it is something to wish on:
a spark of light.

December 24, 2008

It's almost done, and many things are ending
with this strange year; our spiralling lives appear
to be remarkably in sync with the rending
of the world from its imago, and the fear

Clouding the ancient certainties of blood
and dominion, as invisible pillars crumble
and a strange sickness flowers, bringing a flood
of disease, later plagues of the humble

Sins like greed and hubris, now evolved
into market forces that defeat
the real, whose incantations could dissolve
the solidity of oil and gold and wheat

Into mirages written on toxic paper –
the writs on lives built over centuries
now, by these words, transformed into vapour,
the way your love for me, and memories

Will fade after a time. This diary
is at an end, and I must leave before long,
because the inexorable gyre we
spiral in has reached its point, and this song

Has not changed it, though I remain hopeful, prolix,
seeing us reflected everywhere –
from films and novels to dire economics –
made offerings to the demigods of fear.

And now, the time is here, the start
of the end of life as we have lived it,
because I will fade from your little heart,
for all the love my greed and hubris could give it.

February 14, 2009 (Toronto)

They find me at the oddest times, these moments,
inopportunely, on a crowded train
with my eyes closed, and thinking of a home

that is empty now, but echoes still the ferments
of laughter, kisses withheld, and screams of pain
erupting at the oddest times; those moments

Near bedtime, when a little body, incensed
at the doused television, loudly complained;
with eyes unclosed, thinking of a home

In cheerful primary colours, housing oddments
with names like Pablo, Unuqa and Jane,
they find me at the oddest times, at moments

When the absence in me is so immense
I think of a raft, the sea, relentless rain; ˙
with my eyes closed, and thinking of a home

Protected by an impenetrable fence
and whitewashed walls adorned with crayon stain,
they find me at the oddest times, those moments;
my eyes close, and I know you are my home.

THE LAST AVATAR

(for Lloyd Best)

I

So, say there is something to religious myth,
and bearded committees seasonally sit

in cloudy blue rooms to decide our fate,
our needs, desires, and our progress to date,

but unlike the patriarchs of the yellowed scrolls
or fanatics who die for seventy virgin girls,

our committees are urbane & do not heed
the lurid blood-inked parchments of folly and greed,

or theatres of snowy togas and screedy prayers;
they pierce through these artificial layers,

the spiral algebra of genetics & essence,
and refine the plot of the hidden human sequence,

the thunderous wonders and climatic signs to direct
the ragged multitudes' slow, upward trek

through curvy, beige-skinned deserts, littered with sin,
and led by hirsute shepherds in lion-skin

in search of the date-palm's spiny green sail,
and to protect them from the alpha male –

they whose tinny music and martial parades
stampede the herd from paradise to Hades.

For our committee is not omnipotent;
they are bound by the gods' indulgent covenant,

and are mere ministers in the heavenly See,
advising her moody red-eyed Highness, Kali,

to eschew epic vengeance for moral force,
to guide, or coax, every local resource

to satiate the multitudes' local lust
to mingle bodies with their indigenous dust.

Our place and selves are not ours, their wisdom
goes, till they're claimed in local idiom –

an episteme their efforts could not ingrain,
even in the death throes of Kali's reign.

They tried mystic science, then simple myth,
but the matter stubbornly spurned the spirit,

and new gods emerged in cinematic chapels
debuting in well-plotted, racy gospels –

fables showing youth and beauty as virtues
and Thanatos carved into golden statues;

and Kali's age became terror without purpose,
the most fearsome void in all the cosmos.

II

But before Eschaton, one thing remained
so the flesh would not return to dust in vain.

The age had failed, our arbitrators agreed,
though the tree of life could yet produce a seed.

But the Feuilleton age had left the earth sterile:
the soil was gravelly, tired and leached of will;

its tillers had lost all sense of what could have been
before the harvest of original sin.

Only *deus ex machina* remained,
which course only one authority could arraign,

The mighty Brahma, master of the heavenly mansion;
so our committee composed the final petition.

They stumble in the darkness moaning, they wrote,
not knowing they alone can end their hurt.

The song and wonder of creation are wasted
on those who plug their ears and turn their faces.

We could write a tome on their stupidity
but that would only add futility

to an endless catalogue of grief and deviance
which they season with a blank indifference,

for it seems they have heeded Milton's gospel
and negotiated terms with darkest hell.

Now noise and darkness give them joy and light
and hunger brings them gladness and blindness sight,

and though we cannot deny the mass is lost
we can yet release the jewels from the dross;

so we ask for a last rage of the divine
to turn the poison they drink into wine,

a final divine spark, a Promethean flare,
to show how flimsy heaven's barriers are,

so we might at least end this wretched age
in the shape of a divine after-image.

Brahma considered this; already the age
had consumed its pantheon; every rishi, sage

and demigod bearing wisdom and heavenly graces
had traversed deserts and sat in the dark places,

but to no avail; the world remained evil and churning,
its deserts growing, its face cracked and burning.

Now all that remained in the blue-roomed city
were the jaded architects of eternity:

Vishnu, Shiva, and He, whose stately stasis
had kept creation from its moment of crisis;

but He knew that Kali's tantrums could shake heaven
and decided, sighing, that the triad should waken

and descend into creation as mere men
to shepherd the flock to its final end.

III

But where to alight in the sorry sphere?
They chose to plough the field that was most bare:

a group of islands near the world's navel
where the cord binding life had not yet unravelled.

The islands' many-hued votaries were unique,
the descendants of the eternal meek

who the committee for old mythologies
had never considered in its theologies.

Rather than the blue-eyed superman,
their hero was a swarthy everyman,

a lamb revisionists had cast as star
over the lion from the house of Judah,

whose salvation drama would require
an empty stage, outside the ancient mire

of low technology and iron tradition,
to cure the old world of inanition,

to shed its stifling outer carapace
of hierarchic tribe and church and caste,

enrobed in purple and rooted in the primeval,
and whose pale inner purpose remained survival.

The plan was to trade this karmic divertissement
for the price of a few centuries' enslavement,

and from this frontier of pain and ambition
would come the seeds and saplings of a new Eden.

But after five violent centuries,
there stood only a theatre of miseries.

The Gangetic peasant and the Bantu slave,
the Chinese coolie and the Eurotrash knave

refused to mingle with the other's dust
(except in the red light of night-time lust),

and reformed their masters' echelons
to breed a litter of coloured Babylons.

The cities became laboratories of vices
where the feel of daily life was crisis.

The peasants, released from the ancient prison,
could never unlearn the comfort of submission

to the genetic thrall of the alpha male
who promised from his bucket would come the Grail.

And with each passing generation they increased
their pain, and finally made it a feast —

a yearly carnival of noise and delusion
which became their mockery of salvation.

They dressed themselves in masks and armour
and screamed out hymns in a violent clamour.

Some were half-serious, and half in despair,
half hoping, half praying someone would hear

the screams and recognize the terror in them
as the fearful frenzy of abandoned children.

And it was here that our triumvirate
descended, each at a different place and date,

but each journey mirrored the larger intent
to enter the world through the line of the peasant —

the best of the mongrel races, who still retained
a sunlit dream of the world, for which they trained

their sons, and aimed them for its centre, to follow
a path ancestral pasts would never allow:

to break the ties of *jati*, Porro, and blood,
and reach nobility, even demi-godhood,

to bask in disgruntled subjects' heresies
who resent the scale of the larger verities,

and resist stories, songs or learned discourses
that remind them of their magnificent smallness.

IV

The plan produced paradox in consequence;
this was the first time the three had come at once

and the fragile atoms of the lower strata
shattered from the force of divine matter.

Euclid's dimensions collapsed beneath the souls
and divine shards were strewn through the three worlds,

creating premature hybrids of gods and men
and causing irruptions of unworldly doctrine:

the Absurd, the Surreal, flower power, the Marxists,
and clusters of genius in the island nexus:

Lewis, Williams, Minshall, Harris and James –
and the lesser lights with unremarkable names

who emerged from our triad's incipience
suffused with a heaven-scented immanence.

So from a history measured in tortoise shells
the narratives now mimicked bounding gazelles.

The earthbound human trajectory had altered
so much in the etheric wake of the triad

that wonders mocking sanguine scholastic logic
emerged from the chasm between science and magic,

and seraphic spirit infused human means
to recreate the ethereal machines

which speckled the darkness of a banausic age
with rages of techno-cosmic persiflage –

the ether which pervades the upper worlds
and allows the communion of higher souls

was emanated below as cyberspace
through whose worldwide mazes its webbing laced

the body of the miserable masses
to their disembodied heads and fellow vassals

and transubstantiated an alien spirit
into a place and time not made for it.

The masses were wired for medieval dogma
and desired little more than the promised soma;

the idea of the semi-divine cyborg
replacing the semi-lunatic thaumaturge

was heresy to the god-fearing prole
who despaired at an over-complex world.

The ethos this strange fusion came to embody
veered between violence and comedy

whose existence was outlawed by its saviours
since the committee's laws were also nature's.

Into this miasma of cosmic confusion
descended the last comedy of redemption.

V

Shiva was born into a lion's house,
a Brahmin votive to a past which doused

its supplicants in ritual cruelty
as a means to prove the *chela's* fealty

to the memory of a past of heroes and myths
which Shiva adjudged an Area of Darkness.

In eighteen years he etched each image and accent
of every corner of his brown internment –

the brassy water urns and the prayer gongs,
and the low voices singing Indian film songs –

and saw, in the last days of the dark age,
the players lose the divine plot, and the stage

become a yellow Babel of base desire,
a decadent taunt to Kali's destructive ire,

and wondered how these *shudras* had got so far
without their gods to tell them who they were.

And Shiva saw that clarity and truth
might cure the malaise from the rotting root.

He taught them history, myth, and common-sense
and showed them the lessons of their innocence

from pristine El Dorado, through first arrival,
through guerilla wars and enigmas of survival;

Shiva traced the path from mud to mortar,
but the multitudes refused to cross the border

from hut to house, from the primal velleity
to the pulverizing roar of modernity.

Vishnu, ever the mediator, remained
undecided; he could not be constrained

to a single line of descent or tradition
and chose to begin in the heart of division –

a splinter of green insignificance
from the old contretemps of Britain and France

whose warring ships and roaring cannons had rotted,
but whose people and landscape remained besotted,

torn between tongues, and divided to the vein,
no thing could be contained in a single name –

the lives divided between force and memory
into daylight and night-time words and history;

the days in an Imperial pastoral,
the green nights in dreams of the ancestral

unfolded in the patois of the slave Shabine,
from mouths that begged their God to save the Queen.

And Vishnu, the divided child of high browns,
came to master his people's inner songs

and became, as John to Patmos, the legislator
of the black, mournful hills, the sole relater

of the tribes' hidden dreams, and the grey, shapeless
longing for wholeness that afflicted the hopeless.

He became the amanuensis of an old rage,
the dramatist for the tragedy of the age

which began and ended in the endless sea,
as all epics begin and end, in monody —

the single song at the edge of history's knife
that carves the wretched one or another life.

But by the end of their lifetime's travail
the duo's civilizing mission had failed.

This left only Brahma, the last of the triad,
the final hope of the heavenly myriad.

The stoic committees had made their notes in silence
and had looked on in stony ambivalence

with the coolness of the white-robed scientist
measuring the death throes of the fittest,

or extracting the minute measurements
of the primal atom excited to violence.

And, descending, Brahma knew that he
could never hope to defeat futility;

he did not glean his knowledge from above
but came to understand the world through love.

Wisdom came through the dirt beneath his feet
as he walked alone through the lowest street,

and stopped before the heavy iron gate
that no light or thought or hope could penetrate,

to bless the writhing, pain-contorted faces
and softly commit them to the peaceful places.

He sighed at the first childish generations
born out of chains and into new nations,

led by those who, imbued with the sparks rent
from the fabric of heaven at the triad's descent,

believing their accident to be design,
assumed the authority of the divine;

and after a generation of evil and failure
had become high priests of necrophilia;

like farmers who celebrated the absence of rain,
the pretenders transformed virtue into pain,

and Brahma knew at the end of seventy years
that nothing could be gained from grief or tears

but this was the final blessed end of toil,
the welcome shedding of the mortal coil,

and the bright vistas of each evolving fantasia
were sharpened by the silky skein of amnesia –

the committees' final gift to their charges
as they drifted upward on their weary barges.

Salvation was just a game of the immortals
played to amuse themselves in the starry portals.

NOTES TO *HERE*

page 12:

This reference to the *Cabots* and the *Lodges* ("And this is good old Boston,/The home of the bean and the cod,/Where the Lowells talk only to Cabots,/And the Cabots talk only to God"), the Boston *Brahmins*, was intended as a T.S. Eliot allusion, though it appears that I imagined it, since I can't find the poem it came from. If this imagined poem existed, it would make the Sweeney (Apeneck Sweeney) reference a few lines down more obvious.

page 14:

Samadhi, a state of union with the godhead, usually arrived at through meditation. A *havan* is a Hindu prayer ritual which involves a offering (usually fruits, sweetmeats, or sugar) burned in cow-butter. A *bhajan* is a Hindu prayer song, or hymn. The *Manas* is a colloquial name for the *Ramcharitmanas*, a later version of the *Ramayana* by the 16th century Indian poet Tulsidas, which indentured labourers brought with them to the West Indies.

page 15:

Yagnas and *satsanghs* are events in Hindu villages where villagers gather sometimes for religious ceremonies, and/or to hear verses from the *Ramayana*, or the *Vedas*, recited and expounded upon by pundits. The occasions are also used for secular political and social discussions. A *leela* is a story, i.e., the Ramleela, the story of Ram, dramatized or read out. The *Ramleela* in Trinidad is the re-enactment of the *Ramayana* in villages through out the country.

Hema Malini and *Mumtaż* were Bollywood actresses of the 1960s and 1970s, and *Amitabh* alludes to the Bombay movie actor Amitabh Bachchan, the angry young man of Hindi cinema of the 1970s.

Bharat refers to ancestral India.

page 17:

Samajist, refers to the Arya Samaj, the reformist Hindu movement that attracted Mohan Biswas in V.S. Naipaul's *A House for Mr Biswas*.

It was monotheist, opposed to idol worship and, in principle at least, opposed to the hereditary caste system. Several strains of Hinduism exist in Trinidad. The Sanatanists are orthodoxy, the Samajists are a reform movement, somewhat, but not entirely, similar to the Catholic and Protestant churches. Of course, they/we all look alike to the Creole world.

page 19:
Rakshas are the Hindu equivalent of demons. A *sanyasi* is a holy beggar. *Samsara*: the cycle of death and rebirth.

page 20:
Sai Baba is a 20th century Hindu mystic, from India, who some claimed to be an avatar of one of the gods, who had many followers in Trinidad. The later accusations of Sai's (alleged) child abuse and charlatanism hardly registered among the faithful, as in other faiths.

and killed their wives: this was one of the stereotypes of the earlier indentured period that had more than a grain of truth. In a situation of huge imbalance in the proportions of the sexes (at least twice as many men as women), the tendency of at least some women to pursue their economic interests, some men took the law into their own hands and killed or maimed their wives and partners when they left or threatened to leave the marriage.

page 21:
The *frozen marble face* refers to the statue of the Virgin in Presentation College, Chaguanas. *Our Holy Father Narcissus*, refers to the first prime minister of Trinidad and Tobago, Dr Eric Williams who is considered to be (for better or worse) the father of the nation. The narcissism is hardly considered by his admirers who are extremely successful posing as historians and literary scholars. I would have preferred to use the word Fascist, but I needed the rhyme.

page 26:
Ravan is the antagonist, a demon king, in the Ramayana.

page 88:

who promised from his bucket would come the Grail is an allusion to Eric Williams' famous promise: "Here I will let down my bucket", when he came back to Trinidad to become a politician, and was elected to the office of Messiah, which he held until his death.

page 89:

a *Porro* is a West African secret society for men, which reputedly came over to the New World with slavery. All ethnic groups in Trinidad had such societies, which persist to the present day.

ABOUT THE AUTHOR

Raymond Ramcharitar is a Trinidadian poet, playwright, fiction writer and media and cultural critic. He was educated at the University of the West Indies, St Augustine, where he was awarded a BSc in Economics, a Master's in Literatures in English and a Doctorate in Cultural History. He was also awarded a fellowship to Boston University's Creative Writing Programme in 2000 by Nobel Laureate, Derek Walcott, where he studied poetry and drama.

Ramcharitar's published works include academic and creative books and articles. His *The Island Quintet*, published by Peepal Tree in 2009, was shortlisted for the Commonwealth Writers Prize for Best First Book 2010, for the Caribbean & Canada. His collection of poems, *American Fall*, was also published by Peepal in 2007, and a book of media criticism, *Breaking the News, Media & Culture in Trinidad*, was published by Lexicon, in Trinidad in 2005.

His play, "Paradiso", was one of three winners of the British Warehouse Theatre's International Playwriting Festival in 2002.

His doctoral thesis ("The Hidden History of Trinidad: Underground Culture in Trinidad, 1870-1970") set out to challenge the largely ethnocentric historical narratives of West Indian nationalist historians. He has published revisionist academic articles on culture and tourism, literary criticism, and history in journals and edited collections.

He has lectured in Theatre arts, Cultural Studies, and Literature as an adjunct at the University of the West Indies, St Augustine, and works presently as a Communications Consultant in Trinidad. He started writing as a journalist in 1991, working with the *Trinidad Guardian*.

ALSO BY RAYMOND RAMCHARITAR

American Fall
ISBN: 9781845230432; pp. 72; 2007; Price: £7.99

Raymond Ramcharitar's sophisticated and formally ambitious poems have Trinidad as their centre but are global in scope. This is reflected both in their subject matter and their form. The regular movement between the Caribbean, Europe and North America that several of the poems chart is seen both as a contemporary reality, and as no more than a continuation of history's patterns: of, for instance, Indo-Trinidadians who are the 'scions of waylaid Brahmins and pariahs'. This particular migration is placed in the context of a wider world of human movement and 'new theologies springing from old longings'. In form, too, the poems refuse to be confined by any limiting sense of the contemporary and the Caribbean. Use of the archetypes of classical mythology, traditional verse patterns (such as the villanelle) and the careful, confident use of rhythm and rhyme are the most evident outward features of Ramcharitar's concern with form. There are homages to Derek Walcott and Wallace Stevens, but the closer one's acquaintance with the poems, the more evident that Ramcharitar's post-modern voice is a thoroughly individual one, with a capacity for writing verse narratives that are condensed but reverberate like the best short stories, dramatic monologues that skilfully create other voices, and lyric poems that get inside the less obvious byways of emotion.

The Island Quintet: Five Stories
ISBN: 9781845230753; pp. 232; pub.: 2009; price: £8.99

Raymond Ramcharitar's vision is rooted in Trinidad, but as a globalised island with permeable borders, frequent birds of passage, and outposts in New York and London. One of the collection's outstanding qualities is that it is both utterly contemporary and written with a profound and disturbed sense of the history that shapes the island. As befits fiction from the home of carnival and mas', it is a collection much concerned with the flesh – often in transgressive forms as if characters are driven to test their boundaries – and with the capacity of its characters to reinvent themselves in manifold, and sometimes outrageous disguises. One of the masks is race, and the stories are acerbically honest about the way tribal loyalties distort human relations. Its tone ranges from the lyric – Trinidad as an island of arresting beauty – to a seaminess of the most grungy kind. It has an ambition that challenges a novel such as V.S. Naipaul's *The Mimic Men*, but is written with the anger and the compassion of a writer for whom the island still means everything. In the novella, "Froude's Arrow", Ramcharitar has written a profound fiction that tells us where the Caribbean currently is in juxtaposing the deep, still to be answered questions about island existence (the fragmentations wrought by history, the challenges of smallness in the global market, race and class divides) and the scrabbling for survival, fame and fortune that arouse the ire of Ramcharitar's acerbic and satirical vision.